MANTRA MEDITATION

Sounds True, Inc., Boulder CO 80306
© 2004 Thomas Ashley-Farrand

Published 2004
Printed in Korea

ISBN 1-59179-177-4

Audio learning programs by Thomas Ashley-Farrand from Sounds True:
Beginner's Guide to Mantras
Mantra Meditation for Creating Abundance
Mantra: Sacred Words of Power
Mantra Meditation for Attracting and Healing Relationships
Mantra Meditation for Physical Health
The Power of Mantras
Thomas Ashley-Farrand's Healing Mantras

Thomas Ashley-Farrand
NAMADEVA

MANTRA MEDITATION
Change Your Karma with the
Power of Sacred Sound

SOUNDS TRUE

Acknowledgements

Liz Williams, my agent and friend, has my gratitude for her insightful advice on a variety of projects. This book is really her doing from beginning to end. Thank you so much, Liz. But it would also not be completed with such attention to detail without the care of Sounds True Producer and Editor Randy Roark. I am grateful for his commitment to quality and the ease he creates in the process.

There are people who contribute in quiet, but extremely important ways. First, my wife Margalo can take credit for all the books and audio products I have been able to complete. Without her support in a variety of ways, it is improbable that I would have written any books at all. Her love is an ongoing inspiration. Joseph Morales, my webmaster, has contributed countless hours of page design, graphic design, and schedule posting for www.sanskritmantra.com. In fact, the Web site was his original idea. I had no idea what a Web site was in 1996. I am very, very grateful. I also want to express my gratitude to Theresa Van Zante of WMS Media, Marketing and Management, LLC, for her skillful and tireless publicity work, of which I have been the happy recipient.

Lastly, of course, my late spiritual teacher and benefactor, Sadguru Sant Keshavadas, told me many years ago that I would be writing books and teaching. I am amazed as well as more grateful than I can adequately express. His widow, Guru Mata, continues his spiritual work with great humility. Fortunate are we who can spend time with her now and then.

TABLE OF CONTENTS

Introduction   *1*

Chapter 1   6
*The Varieties and Goals
of Meditation Practice*

Chapter 2   12
Our Spiritual Physiology

Chapter 3   18
Taking Control of Your Destiny

Chapter 4   26
The Four Aims of Human Life

Chapter 5   32
*Conducting Your
Mantra Discipline*

Chapter 6   42
Mantras for Artha, or Abundance

Chapter 7   48
*Mantras for Kama,
or Fulfillment of Desires*

Chapter 8   54
Mantras for Upholding Dharma

Chapter 9   64
*Mantras for Moksha,
or Liberation*

Chapter 10   70
*A Feng Shui Mantra for
Clearing Negative Energies*

Chapter 11   74
*Beginning Your First
Mantra Practice*

Chaper 12   76
Good Fortune to You

Bibliography   79

Introduction

WE ARE CUSTODIANS of great power, but we do not think about it or sometimes even believe it. To most of us, power is something that exists outside of ourselves, and no one seems to have control over the events and conditions of his or her life. It can be an internal condition, a relationship, a chain of events, an organization ... there is always something out of our control.

Complicating matters, there is little in the way of reference material—spiritual or otherwise—that explains what tangible, accessible power really is or how to get it. To be sure, there are many self-help books that show us how to control our habits, and develop new and better ones. There are also books that instruct us how to communicate more effectively, and build better personal and business relationships. But nowhere are there clearly defined and explained texts that tell us how we can have an immediate, powerful effect on our environment through the application of some kind of personal force.

In the West, we are not at all accustomed to the idea of having a personal force or power. We are well aware of the power of government and other institutions. We respect and even admire the brute force of machines that power our economy. We are all becoming better informed through the power of mass media, but it, more than anything else, can convince us that real power lies outside of us. In fact, in the West we are faced with a de facto conditioning that all power is really external to the individual. Part of the lure of the computer is that it increases our sense of personal power and our impact on the world, but for all of its tremendous advantages, it is still external.

In the East, the idea of personal power has been commonly accepted for centuries. It is a paradox that, while there is great poverty in many Eastern nations, there is also a history and legacy of great spiritual power from Rama, Krishna, the Buddha, and others. Like Western religious leaders, these Eastern figures stated clearly that whatever they have attained, we can also attain. There are, of course, many different methods taught for accumulating personal power for spiritual and material advancement. The one that has been taught to me and that I present in this book is mantra meditation.

Mantra meditation is not only something one practices, but a radical re-envisioning of ourselves, our lives, and our ability to create the future we desire. The principles of mantra meditation are based on a classical Eastern model of how the universe operates, and our place and purpose in it. In this model, the universe is composed of energy, and the most important thing we can do in order to manifest the kind of life we want is to tap into that energy, specifically in this case through the power of sound.

Through the application of Sanskrit spiritual formulas, energy comes into our body that dissolves our difficulties and improves our lives. Over time—sometimes many lives—our *karma*, which is a term I discuss in more detail a bit later—becomes exhausted, and we become spiritually free of any worldly bondage. Then we are presented with a new set of options as evolving entities.

Among the many mantras that have been recorded by sages and mystics, some of which have come to the West, I have selected and categorized a few that are the most useful in pursuing the classical Eastern aims of human existence: prosperity, worldly desires, ethical and noble development, and spiritual fulfillment leading to liberation. Those goals are explained in subsequent chapters, but for now, know that with mantras you can begin to shape the outer manifestations of your life.

So powerful are these ancient tools that they were intentionally hidden by the Brahman priesthood in India for centuries. It is only in the last century that the lid has come off, and teachers have come from India and Tibet to share their spiritual wealth with students in the West, many of them their former students from previous lives. Collectively, this spiritual work will ultimately reshape the planet, but in the short term, you can fulfill some of your most cherished desires and have a better life.

Mantra meditation is not magic, but the results can be magical. Through the practice of a daily discipline that is simple and easy to use—customarily over a period of forty days—anyone can learn how to organize some of the fundamental energies of the universe to directly affect their specific concerns.

People have healed themselves or family members using mantra as a tool to guide them to proper practitioners and methods. New relationships have appeared, satisfying long-standing desires. Better jobs have been secured, raises obtained, and working conditions improved, all by harnessing the great power in Sanskrit mantras that activates the dynamic forces within each and every one of us.

In this program, I have collected some the most popular and effective mantras, and presented them in such a way that you can begin practicing mantra meditation immediately. You do not have to travel to India, or become a monk, or change your religion in order to come to a new understanding of the basic principles of causality and to use them to get the results you desire.

I have also included a chapter on a space-cleansing *Feng Shui* mantra from the Chinese system for organizing the space environments in our lives for maximum benefit. Some have suggested that Feng Shui derives from the ancient Hindu science of *Vastu*. Certainly the underpinning philosophies are nearly identical, but there are functional differences, just as there are among various schools of Feng Shui. When I met Fung Shui Master Nathan Batoon, I was struck by his humility as well as his expertise. He and I share a connection through the *Vajrayana* branch of Tibetan Buddhism, so the type of Feng Shui from which I have selected this mantra is called *Black Hat* (Vajrayana-based) Feng Shui. Since we all live and work in various environments, I thought it important to include a mantra that would cleanse the spaces that you inhabit.

Before you can most successfully practice mantra meditation, you need to understand some of the important principles of this system. Thus, the first section of this program prepares the ground for your practice by explaining the basic principles underlying the use of mantras. This includes an introduction to some of the forces of this system as personified in the Hindu pantheon of gods and goddesses, because most of the mantras you will be using will be directed to these figures, included in the classical Eastern scriptures from which these mantras have been preserved.

The second part of the book provides specific mantras for goals, objectives, and desires. The CD included with this program will help you with pronunciation of the individual mantras. Since these mantras are based on sacred sounds tuned to primordial energies, it is important to pronounce mantras as correctly as possible, since it is through the repetition of these sounds that you will be tuning your mind, body, and spirit to the underlying cosmic vibrations that most closely resonate with your intended outcome. You can chant with the CD, out loud or silently. Both silent and audible chanting are powerful, so do that which appeals to you. You can also, of course, just listen or chant while you are doing anything else. I listen to CDs while driving; if you do, please be safety-minded while you listen.

Although the focus of this program is on improving various aspects of the "Four Aims of Human Life," the ultimate goal of mantra practice is spiritual freedom. Mantra meditation will deepen your connection with your essential divine self. You will learn how to quiet the mind, entering into ever-deeper levels of silence. There, mysteries of life and the universe are revealed, bringing sublime satisfaction and peace.

As in any spiritual discipline, the most important aspect of mantra meditation is regular practice. Mantra meditation—or any meditation practice—will rarely have dramatic results if only practiced occasionally. A classical mantra practice is typically forty days in length. You can, of course, practice your mantra as often or as infrequently as you like, but for best results, you should do the forty-day discipline as classically practiced for thousands of years. Discipline places the key in the lock, and regularity turns the key.

Since coming to the West Coast in 1982, I have taught successive chanting workshops, each seven years in length, where I organized and refined methods for teaching mantra meditation. Since then, I have taught people not only in workshops, but through books and audio programs, how to actively work to change conditions in their lives through mantra-based spiritual disciplines. The results come to me every day through email from around the world. As one voice, they speak the truth of mantra meditation: "You can change your life. You are endowed with great power to help yourself and the world."

CHAPTER
ONE

The Varieties and Goals of Meditation Practice

MOST OF US ARE familiar with the common practices of meditation—from the Christian tradition of contemplating sacred scripture or a particular concept or quality, to the breath-centered practices of Buddhism, to the postures of *Hatha Yoga* and other yogic disciplines. All of these methods are valuable, and they all work in different ways to deepen our ability to connect to various underlying aspects of reality and our experience.

Of course, any of these forms of meditation practiced only once or twice usually will not produce the results you are seeking, but repeated periods of practice with ever-increasing levels of mastery will take you down the road to whatever goal you seek—whether it is a quality of mindfulness in your everyday life, a specific goal or result, or deeper and deeper states of concentration that will eventually lead you to the very source of thought itself.

In the East, all of these are considered forms of meditation practice, not "true meditation." True meditation is defined in Eastern scriptures as doing absolutely nothing except Being. In true meditation, thought ceases and, because nature abhors a vacuum, the mind begins to work in a different way. So difficult is it to explain a non-verbal functioning of the mind, that we have words like *mystical* that really only hint at the possibilities. In Buddhism, the term *zen* comes close to this state of mind that is conscious and aware, but works in a way different from the way most us live our lives. In the East, prayer is what we do when we talk to God, and true meditation is what happens when we listen—to the universe, to our own divinity, to God.

But many of us are most comfortable when we feel we are actually doing something to bring about what we want. Doing nothing is hard, and clearing the mind, or just "being" with our eyes open or closed while doing nothing, is almost impossible. That is why, over the centuries, various forms of spiritual practices have been perfected to quiet the mind so that true meditation can take place, and one of the oldest spiritual practices is known as mantra meditation.

MANTRA MEDITATION

For thousands of years, the use of genuine Sanskrit mantras and spiritual formulas has been practiced in order to work in very specific ways to reduce karma and to attune our minds, bodies, and spirits to the various invisible energies that exist in the universe. Systematic work with mantras also deepens our breath and automatically increases our ability to concentrate. As the mind becomes clearer, new kinds of perceptual information appear to us as our outer awareness expands. Inner awareness also grows as our karmic struggles are burned away through the repetition of these ancient sacred formulas. We begin to see in new ways, hear in new ways, and understand in new ways.

The word *mantra* is derived from two Sanskrit words. The first is *manas* or "mind," and the second syllable is drawn from the Sanskrit word *trai*, which means "to protect" or "to free from." Therefore, a mantra is a tool, used by the mind, that eventually frees us from the vagaries of the mind.

Repeating any sound produces an actual physical vibration. Nowhere is this idea truer than in Sanskrit mantra. When chanted out loud or silently, mantras create a single, powerful vibration that corresponds to both a specific spiritual energy frequency and also a state of consciousness in seed form. Over time, the mantra process begins to override and absorb all of the other smaller vibrations that eventually become subsumed within the mantra. After a length of time that varies from individual to individual, the great wave of the mantra overwhelms all other vibrations. Ultimately, when practiced repeatedly, the mantra will result in a subtle change of state in the organism, where the organism vibrates at a rate in tune with the energy and spiritual state represented by and contained within the mantra. Just as a laser is light that is coherent in a new way, the person who becomes one with the state produced by the mantra is also coherent in a way that did not exist prior to the conscious undertaking of repetition of the mantra.

When a mantra is chanted over a long period of time, the power of the mantra overcomes all of the other vibrations operating in the mind. The first level of this is that the mantra manifests itself in some sort of vision or form to indicate that one has stilled the other vibrations. Then, with continued mantra work, the mind becomes completely still. Now another spiritual dynamic comes into play that the mystics are hard pressed to explain, because the mind now begins to work in a different way. Some yogis may describe it as "Realization"; the Zen Buddhists as "Nirvana." The *Jnanis*, or seekers after knowledge, describe it as the beginning of true knowledge—which is quite different from "information" that we may get from books. What all of these and other descriptions have in common is that the state of the mind is different and evades ordinary description.

Another aspect of a mantra involves the intention of its use. If the actual physical vibration is coupled with a mental intention, the vibration then contains an additional mental component that influences the result of repeating it. In this way, the sound of the mantra is the carrier wave and the intent is overlaid upon the waveform, just as a colored gel influences the appearance and effect of a white light.

The mantras and practices detailed in this program will all help you achieve deeper concentration, mental clarity, a quieter inner world, a calmer inner environment, and help you plough through your karmic barriers, obstacles, and conditions. Chanting these mantras will also help you to fulfill your desires and lead you toward spiritual fulfillment.

It is in their ability to fulfill desires and promote health and well-being that mantras will prove their value to you without persuasion from me or anyone else. Also, by helping you to solve some of life's problems and difficulties, you will be simultaneously be moving forward spiritually toward realization of your true divine nature. This is why any mantra practice—no matter the goal—will become a "can't lose" situation. You can help yourself in specific situations while, at the same time amassing excellent spiritual fringe benefits, until you finally reach the ultimate goal of all spiritual practices—attainment of a state of true listening, of solely Being, of "true meditation."

THE SOURCE OF MANTRAS

Two ancient Eastern spiritual texts present in-depth explorations of the Sanskrit language, one of the earliest known forms of human language. The first of these, the *Laksmi Tantra*, explains the construction of the universe, in specific Eastern spiritual terms, from its first conception as pure energy, to the creation of the material universe, known as the Earth Plane. It also includes a variety of mantra practices designed to achieve various states of consciousness in attunement with the divine.

The other text, the *Siva Sutras*, was revealed to a sage who was directed to it in meditation, after it had mystically appeared carved in stone. The *Siva Sutras* consist of a discussion of the nature and states of consciousness and energy, as well as methods of spiritual evolution.

Amazingly, the chapters in both scriptures that discuss Sanskrit are so similar that they are almost identical—interchangeable, really. The gist of what they convey is that the universe at the physical and subtle level is composed of fifty principal vibrations. Collectively, these sound vibrations are called the *Matrika*—The Mother. These sounds exist in three categories 1) audible sound, 2) subtle sound, and 3) completely silent (yet existent) sound. These three categories make up the *spanda* (vibrations) that have constructed the universe we inhabit.

From the *Laksmi Tantra*

The ultimate (absolute) imperishable Brahman, undifferentiated between (polarization of) knowledge and agent appearing in the form of ever-shining light and identical with the All is termed *Aham* (I). Its ever active *Shakti* is the I-hood identified with it and appears as indistinguishable light ... [T]his same Shakti ... then evolves out of the Great God into *Shabdabrahma* (Divine Sound or *Spanda*) ... Consider this unmanifested eternal sound as resembling the faint sound of a musical instrument ... *Matrika* is the collective term for all the letters or sound units which are called the Mother or Matrika because they form the basis or source of all the *lokas* (planes of existence) ... The Matrika is the source of all mantras.

From this point forward, the *Laksmi Tantra* explains in detail the various letters of the Sanskrit alphabet and their function in the construction of our reality.

From the *Siva Sutras*

She [the Matrika] is the Shakti of the creator of the world and is said to be in constant and intimate union with Him ... [T]his Shakti appears as the entire universe in the form of the Matrika composed of fifty letters ... [As the source of them] the mantras resorting to that power of Spanda (divine sound, also known as Shabdabrahma) proceed to perform their respective functions, even as the senses of the embodied ones do ... The source of all mantras is the divine I-consciousness and it is to this divine I-consciousness that all mantras [ultimately] are directed.

From this point on, the *Siva Sutras* also presents the letters of the Sanskrit alphabet in detail as to their spiritual state and function. The central thesis is that the Sanskrit alphabet is the collection of vibrations that has constructed the whole universe. It is this conception of the Sanskrit alphabet from which the mantras we will learn have been created.

CHAPTER
TWO

Our Spiritual Physiology

PARAMAHANSA YOGANANDA, author of *Autobiography of a Yogi* and the well-known Eastern sage who brought the *Kriya Yoga* technique to the West, used to sing in one of his songs to the divine, "Thousands of suns and moons in my body do shine." Mystics and experienced meditators will tell you he meant this literally. From his experience, he understood that everything in the universe can be accessed by going within. The vehicle for accessing all of this is the *chakra system*, specifically the six principal chakras along the spine in the *subtle body*.

Chakra translates literally as "wheel." In yogic philosophy, chakras are described as energy-processing centers in the *subtle body*—an energy body that interpenetrates the physical body. The subtle body is sometimes called the *Astral Body*, but the term *Etheric Body* is more accurate.

The existence of these wheel-shaped, spinning vortices along the spine is well established in nearly all Sanskrit-based spiritual texts. Although there are actually dozens of chakras in the subtle body, the principle ones discussed in mainstream Eastern spiritual texts are six in number, and are located along the spine, with a seventh at the top of the head.

Each of the chakras located on the spine has a different number of spokes. The one at the brow center has two spokes, while the one at the bottom of the spine has four. Others have twelve, sixteen, and so forth. If all of the spokes of the six wheels

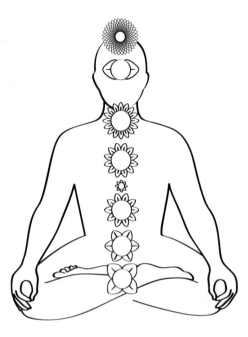

are added together, they total fifty. These fifty spokes contain the vibrations of the building blocks of the entire universe—the *Matrika*, or the map of the sounds of creation described earlier.

What this means for all of us, and particularly those of us who practice mantra meditation, is that all of the energy of the universe that we need to fulfill our desires is as close as—and is actually identical with—our own bodies.

In addition to our chakras, there is also a power cell at the base of the spine, feminine in nature, known as the *kundalini shakti*. It powers everything we do, including our thoughts, actions, and all the physical activity of our bodies, whether awake or asleep. Usually, we barely touch its potential power, although advanced yogis and spiritual adepts have learned various techniques to use shakti energy to perform superhuman feats. These abilities are due to their superior knowledge of the power of the universe at every level of manifestation—non-physical as well as physical. Yet shakti lies even beyond every level of manifestation. It is the primordial power behind creation, that is never depleted or exhausted even as it creates everything and brings everything to its end. If the Matrika is the stone and mortar of all creation, shakti is the guiding skill and intelligence of the mason who puts everything together.

ACCESSING THE MATRIKA

The Matrika is all around us and inside us, all the time, but just as the rays that carry the information for our televisions, radios, and cell phones need a piece of equipment designed to turn these invisible rays into perceptible information, we need an instrument that can translate these invisible waves of ambient energy into a useable form.

For spiritual energy, the instrument to tune into this energy is known as the *subtle body*. Since all of the vibrations existing in the physical and non-physical universe are also constructed in the chakras in the subtle body, we might say that access to the Matrika—in the form of the Sanskrit alphabet—is hard-wired into us. Of course, most of us are completely unaware or only dimly aware of this, so mostly our equipment remains unused.

There are also other ways of accessing this ambient spiritual energy. Different kinds of spiritual practices are designed to tap into the energy according to their varying spiritual technologies. *Pranayama* (scientific breathing), Hatha Yoga, prayer, certain kinds of ecstatic dance, various types of devotional singing, or chanting can all access aspects or layers of this spiritual energy, but in this discussion, I will limit my discussion to its use via Sanskrit mantra.

When we chant one of the ancient spiritual formulas, the sounds in the mantra cause certain petals of the chakras to vibrate in specific ways. The result is that, as the petals vibrate, they pull in tiny amounts of the ambient energy. By chanting, we are increasing the total amount of spiritual energy available for our use. Paramahansa Yogananda wrote about this process in his book *Autobiography of a Yogi* as increasing the wattage of our spiritual bulbs.

KARMA

The Buddha taught that whenever we decide to solve any problem or condition, we must start where we are. It is also taught in the East that we came into this life with certain mental, emotional, and situational karmic predispositions. For that reason, before one can best begin a process of mantra meditation, we must first begin with an understanding of *karma*.

The concept of karma is based upon the idea that an individual will, over time, incarnate many times in different bodies. In this process, we will come back as different sexes, as different races, and with different physical and mental gifts and defects for the purpose of clearing our karmic obligations, until we have finally purified ourselves completely.

Karma operates through the Law of Cause and Effect. In other words, what we have sown in this or other lifetimes will inevitably bear fruit in either this life or a future life. In any moment, we are free to make any kind of decision we choose within the scenarios of our chosen life situation, and these decisions will increase or lessen our karmic burden.

Since most of us have accumulated a large amount of karma, it is usually not possible to work all of it off in a single lifetime. This means that we choose, before coming to Earth, the circumstances in which we will work off a specific amount of karmic obligation, even though we usually do not arrive with any conscious understanding of our karmic affairs.

In a particular lifetime, some of us may also have the great karmic good fortune to gain the Grace of God through the appearance of a true teacher, saint, sage, guru, or master. This Grace can often accelerate the process of reducing our karmic burden immeasurably in any particular lifetime. Such Grace is usually, but not always, earned through sincere efforts maintained through several lifetimes, but at other times, the mercy of God is nearly causeless.

There is a folk tale from India that describes how karma, grace, and devotion work together to influence our liberation:

One day in a village, a Holy Man was holding *Satsang*—giving a spiritual talk and answering questions—in the town center near a well. At the conclusion of the talk, a wealthy merchant who gave liberally to worthy causes asked the Holy Man how long it would take him to exhaust all of his karma and reach the divine abode. After a moment of contemplation, the Holy Man said that because the merchant had been a very good man for many lifetimes, it would only be twelve lifetimes before he had a sacred vision of the divine beloved and achieved freedom from all of his karma. The merchant was overjoyed and thanked the Holy Man profusely.

Then a wandering mendicant who lived only on alms and the kindness of strangers asked the same question. The Holy Man again went within and answered that only three more lifetimes would be required. The mendicant could not believe his ears. "Three more!" he thought, "That's ridiculous." Out loud he said, "You mean that even after all of the deprivation and suffering I have undergone in this life, I still have to live three more lifetimes?" The Holy Man nodded yes. "Then I'm going to enjoy what time I have left in this one." And he threw down his mendicant's donation basket and began a life devoted to satisfying all of his sensual desires.

Finally, a thief timorously approached the Holy Man and asked the same question. After a brief inner contemplation, the Holy Man pointed to a nearby tall tree and spoke. "You see that tree? Well, as many leaves as there are on that tree, so many lives it will take for you to work out your karma." The thief began to dance in ecstasy and shouted out in joy, "How compassionate is God! After all the bad things I've done, God still gives me a chance to reach Him and it will only take that many lifetimes? Oh, how fortunate I am!" At that moment, the Grace of the Supreme manifested, and the thief achieved *moksha*, or spiritual liberation, on the spot. The intense and pure devotion of the thief in that moment had invoked the Grace of God, and his mountain of karma was instantly burnt to ashes.

As negative karma is cleared—whether through the results of mantra practice, right action, or divine Grace—positive karma is able to flow freely into our lives, desires are fulfilled, and spiritual abilities (or *siddhis*, seemingly magical abilities) manifest. We can become healers. We can become clairvoyant or clairaudient, and we will, as well, have moved another step forward toward moksha, or complete spiritual freedom.

CHAPTER
THREE

Taking Control of Your Destiny

FROM THE TIME we have the faintest glimmer of consciousness, we learn that we can have an effect upon the world around us, at least in terms of getting what we want. We learn that when we cry, we can motivate someone to pick us up, give us food, or change our diapers.

Then, soon after we have assimilated the use of the "crying lever" to get what we want, we discover that different kinds of behavior can get us other things as well. For instance, throwing tantrums, yelling, or throwing objects will often result in our parents getting for us the other things we want. In this way, we arrive at a general understanding that "noise" in some form will often get us the results that our burgeoning egos want.

Then one day we yell, or throw a tantrum, or cry, and something weird happens. Somebody yells back at us or refuses to get us what we want. After several such incidents, we begin to learn that the law of getting what we want is not absolute, and that the same actions can have different results. We might also learn that it is easier to get things in the morning when people are in a hurry or not so tired, or that moms are easier to get things from than dads.

Once we assimilate this new information, we begin to vary our tactics to get what we want as each new variable is presented to us. We can become astonishingly good at controlling our environment and fulfilling our desires.

Of course, complications inevitably appear. For instance, we also learn that other people have their own desires, and will not automatically give us what we want. Sometimes they will even actually oppose us because they want those things themselves. Or they might not even want what we want, but simply do not want us to have it. Now we are exposed to the conflicting desires that operate according to the wide diversity of logic and emotion that is common to living in community with others. Getting what we want becomes a much more complicated process.

Eventually, we arrive at an understanding that is so mind-boggling that we stuff it into our subconscious mind. This new understanding is so powerful that humanity has developed elaborate social and societal fabrics of behavior and interpersonal ritual to mask it so that things do not get out of hand. We even pass laws and construct prisons to enforce the social mores that disguise this truth, while vigorously enforcing artificial barriers that surround it to keep things under control. This truth is that there are no real rules in life at all.

What this means is that you are actually "free" to do anything you want, even if social mores or laws prohibit it. You can, and people often do, murder someone else. You can go out right now and rob a bank. In fact, you can do anything you want at any time.

But even though there are no rules, our actions, decisions, thoughts, feelings, and emotions always have consequences. For instance, if you hit someone, there is every likelihood that they will hit you back. But that does not mean that there is any rule in life which says that hitting someone is not possible, because it is.

A true understanding of this relationship between an action and its consequences shows us that actions have their effects upon our immediate environment. These consequences are as real as any action, and can be felt, experienced, or observed in the universe as a whole, but they are most obvious within our own personal universe.

This is how karma operates in our lives. We ourselves are the primary source of what happens to us, because at some level we are constantly creating our future through our thoughts, emotions, and actions in the present moment.

Contrary to the idea that we are powerless corks tossing on the sea of circumstance, we are actually powerful beings who constantly work to structure and restructure the events in our lives. The more raw, personal power you can apply, the more powerful effects you will create. And once you begin to realize that you are constantly influencing and changing the reality of your life in every moment, you begin to realize the true power of the fact that there are no rules, but only consequences. Finally, you come to understand that the present is largely the result of the consequences of what you have done in the past, and that you are, in actuality, holding your future in your hands.

THE LAWS OF THE UNIVERSE

Although there are no rules concerning behavior, there are, of course, unchangeable aspects to life that apply to everyone and everything alike. For instance, there are rules of nature, such as the law of gravity, which affect us all equally. Gravity applies both to a baby falling out of a crib and an apple falling from a tree. Likewise, the sun always appears each morning in the east and sets each evening in the west. The seasons reappear every year in a certain predictable order. Everything that was born will eventually die. These are the same natural laws that prohibit us from flying with our physical bodies, or walking through walls while in our bodies (unless we become very, very advanced). In this way, although there are no rules governing what we can do within our natural limits, there are often very specific laws that define the possibilities available to us, including our possible behavior.

In addition to these natural laws, there are also those skills that we learn through experience very early in life. We learn, as already explained, that if we know where the proper levers are, we can apply them to get what we want, and that some of these are more likely to get us what we want than others. There may be an ever-increasing complexity of levers and combinations of levers that evades our ability to know them all, but we know they exist and that they work.

We also learn that something will not appear simply because we desire it. There are, in fact, certain things that only a specific, dedicated, and disciplined path of action—a continuous string of decisions coherently structured in a calculated manner to achieve a desired result—will accomplish. Of course, there will be consequences to using some of these levers in a negative way: social punishment, legal punishment, corporate punishment, and the like. We eventually learn that we are completely free to do whatever we want within a wide range of choices, and we also learn that we will be the ultimate beneficiaries of the consequences of our actions.

GOALS CHANGE EVERYTHING

There is only one exception to this rule of no rules, and that is, there are no rules unless you have a specific goal in mind. If you want to obtain a particular goal, then you will be more likely to achieve it if you investigate—and abide by—the various rules that will best increase your chances of obtaining that goal.

In this way, if you have a goal and you are serious about achieving that goal, it stands to reason that you should begin by examining possible rules surrounding its achievement, including potential obstacles that could arise along the way. Next, you might examine the personal and environmental resources that will aid in the accomplishment of your goal. Finally, you should consider aspects of society and its conventions that will aid or detract from gaining your goal. But the drawback to even our most sophisticated analysis is that we can only examine what we can see, what we know, or what seems relevant.

We all know someone who wants to achieve a certain career goal, but has met with one frustration after another. They do everything they can to reach their objectives. They go to school and get the right education, they do the necessary research to learn where the best jobs are, then they learn everything they can about the best ways to interview for a job. They might also network, and even enjoy the support and encouragement of their friends and spouses, but somehow, one opportunity after another ends in disappointment and frustration.

There are others who actually do get the job they desire, only to find that their problems are just beginning. There are problems with their boss, with their associates, with their employees, with their customers, or with the business itself. Nothing seems to go right. And if they eventually leave and find another job, the same problems invariably reoccur.

There are many possible explanations for these types of problems, but the Eastern explanation is that there are subtle but powerful forces at work influencing the situation in invisible ways: karma. But how can we begin to understand these forces of karma if they are, by definition, invisible? The first thing we can do is to examine our underlying assumptions about how our world—and our lives—work.

The first of these would be assumptions about yourself and your life. If you are doing everything you know how to do, and you are still not getting the results you want, there is at least the possibility that your goals are not actually true to your basic nature in some critical way. This means that perhaps your ego-centered desires or your methods for getting what you want may not be in synch with your essential nature—with who you really are.

For most people, it is necessary that your essential nature be the central driving force behind the "creative" aspect of your life. If you have strong ego-based ideas about who you are or who you should be, you can be sure your essential nature will try to undermine any inauthentic ways your ego is conducting your life.

The central problem is often that many of us have been taught to behave, think, and act in ways that are not consonant with who we truly are. Therefore, the first step toward obtaining your goals is to begin by recognizing your inner nature and learning how to live your life in attunement with that inner nature.

Your karma is also an important part of your inner nature, and your karmic patterns will enforce themselves inexorably. Until these contradictory karmic forces are reconciled, you are certain to experience constant and frustrating conflicts that often seem to come out of nowhere, or to repeatedly occur in your life, no matter what you do.

Pursuing our spiritual ideals, any kind of meditation, and keeping a spiritual diary all help us to understand our inner nature, including our karmic propensities. Mantra meditation is also designed to change your karmic condition, as well altering your behavior so as to soften negative karmic patterns and reinforce positive ones. This process will also allow us to get a clear glimpse of the real possibilities inherent in our karma. We can make better choices and establish realistic goals.

Of course, we often have more than one goal—and we also have different kinds of goals. It is also common that at least some of those goals are in conflict with others.

How do we decide what to do when there are conflicting goals? Most of us prioritize and make compromises. We decide that some goals are more important than others, and pursue those first. This is the art of ego-compromise that, from the ego-centered point of view, should work perfectly, but usually only creates new problems.

The first problem is that there may be a negative reaction from the "inner you" to these kinds of compromises. Your inner nature may be in opposition either to one or more of your goals, or to the basic compromise that allows you to go after all of them. Secondly, goals and desires of other people may or may not be in synch with your goals. In fact, some people may have goals and objectives that actually bring them into direct opposition to you. They may want what you have, or they just may not want you to have what you desire, for their own reasons. This is a negative goal for them to have, but it is also a very real force that you will sometimes have to deal with in the world.

Where can we go to learn more about how to attain true happiness and congruence in our lives? Not surprisingly, people have been wrestling with these issues as long as history itself, and many of their answers seem to reside in an area many of us would call spirituality or religion. What the world's spiritual traditions have taught about what is best for all of us individually and collectively is remarkably simple, and it can be summarized in an idea that in the Eastern traditions is known as "The Four Aims of Human Life."

CHAPTER
FOUR

The Four Aims of Human Life

SO FAR WE HAVE TALKED about the fact that are "no rules" in life, and that we have complete freedom of choice, even though we are bound by the karma we are creating through our choices. We have also touched upon something called the "inner you." Needless to say, if there is an "inner you," then we are all surrounded by others, who also have their own "inner you."

In its broadest context, religion has dealt with the formation of rules more than any other institution of humankind. The prescriptions of the Ten Commandments of Moses, the Eightfold Path of the Buddha, the Golden Rule of Christianity, the hundreds of injunctions of the Talmud, the prescriptions of the Holy Koran, the Yamas and Niyamas of Hinduism, and the Do's and Do Nots and the Shoulds and Should Nots of various religions have had more influence on individual and group action than any other single institution, yet throughout time we seem to be wrestling with the same basic problems of how best to live our lives and how to live with others.

The noble goal of these rules is often to help us make decisions that will advance us spiritually. Secondarily, religions also want to help humanity achieve a level of civility that will make life enjoyable for the mass of humanity. The reason these prescriptions have had such a deep and lasting affect on humankind is that our "inner you" has some sense of this, even as our egos attempt to optimize our personal conditions in this particular life.

Even though there seems to be no end to the ego's desires, and the presiding arbiter of our decisions—our ego in concert with our mind—has its own preferences and desires for the things and conditions it wants, the ancient teachings of India say that every individual ego essentially wants the same four things: to be happy always, to be all-powerful, to live forever, and to know everything that can be known.

If you think about it, all of your conscious desires usually fit somewhere into one or more of those categories. If we have health issues, our desire is to be free of them so that we can be happy always: How can we be happy if we are sick or injured? But the desire to be able to overcome all health issues is also partially the desire to be all powerful: If we had true power, we would be able to heal any disease or illness. It can also be seen as a desire to know everything, for true knowledge would allow us to solve any kind of problem, including how to heal ourselves from any malady.

But these teachings also acknowledge that, for anyone except the most highly evolved beings, these four desires, while not impossible, can be frustrating because they are largely out of reach for most of us through our own efforts. The non-attainment of these ego goals seems almost part of natural law.

Once we understand that these four things are unattainable, we often choose to seek more realistic goals—the kind of goals that are not only attainable, but will also bring us in tune with our inner nature and what we truly desire. These kind of goals are what is known in Eastern thought as the "Four Aims of Human Life," or *Artha*, *Kama*, *Dharma*, and *Moksha*.

Artha is wealth in the form of prosperity. Most commonly, this means enough money to live on, to feed our families, or to attain our material goals. *Kama* is the fulfillment of the desires that are most important to us, which can include aspirations to live a happy and satisfying family life with our spouse and children, but can also mean a particular career or social status. *Dharma* is the desire to live in accordance with the divine order—both personal and societal—that keeps the world a just and true place for all people, and to do what we can to keep the world in its proper order. *Moksha* is the desire for liberation or complete spiritual freedom, which is sometimes also called Mukti. This state is achieved when all of one's karma is exhausted, burned up, worked off, or forgiven by God or a divine being with spiritual authority. Once Moksha is attained, one has no more obligations of any kind to this world.

The practice of mantra meditation has been designed to aid in the attainment of all four of these aims or goals of life, including final liberation. It is strongly advised, however, that in order for our goals to be fulfilled, they should be what are called *noble goals*. Used in this way, *noble* means that the various states and items we wish to attain are fair, just, and do no harm to others. For instance, to desire abundance can be a noble undertaking, but there is plenty of money to be made in organized crime, although there is nothing noble about it. In fact, there can be a very undesirable accumulation of bad karma by pursuing our goals by any route available. It is for that reason that all of the mantras given here for abundance include the term *Maha*, which means "heart-centered" in one context, and "great" in another. By focusing our desire in our heart or by calling upon "greatness" in our practice, our efforts will automatically be noble. Make no mistake, the mantras will work whether or not one's goals and methods are noble, but you will only bring about a reduction of your karma if you follow your own innately noble nature.

The mantras included in this book have been organized into sections based on the *Four Aims of Human Life*. Most likely, some of your goals will fall into one or more of the categories.

CREATING A SPIRITUAL DIARY

I am a great believer in spiritual diaries. They help to identify our innermost thoughts and desires. They reveal our cares and fears. They bring up patterns of desire and behavior that can show us where to focus our inner and outer work. If you are so inclined, start a spiritual diary in which you chronicle important events, thoughts, situations, emotions, and your evaluations of them. In a very short period of time, you will begin to see patterns in your inner landscape. It is in these patterns that you can begin to develop priorities for your mantra work. It may be that health issues are clearly foremost, or relationship issues, or ones based in abundance. Seeing your own inner priorities develop, construct a list of objectives that you would like to pursue through mantra. When you have a good idea of what you would like to accomplish, go through the mantras in the following chapters to see which ones apply. It will not take long before you will have laid out several disciplines that may take the next six months to complete. Even if your first layer of objectives takes a year or more to complete, do not concern yourself with how long it might take. Rather ask, "How many lifetimes did it take me to construct this undesirable karma? And look how quickly I can resolve it!"

The bottom line is, you can change your karma. At first, it may appear to be carved in stone, but it is not. With the proper practices, you can change both your outer circumstances and inner conditions.

CHAPTER
FIVE

Conducting Your Mantra Discipline

YOU HAVE A NUMBER of options available to you when deciding to perform a discipline with one or more of the mantras discussed in this book. The discussion here will start with the simplest form of spiritual discipline and move progressively into more arduous practices.

THE FORTY-DAY DISCIPLINE

Important periods of spiritual development involving the number forty occur in most religious traditions. Noah tossed upon the seas for forty days and forty nights. Moses wandered in the wilderness for forty years. Jesus fasted in the desert for forty days. The Buddha provided a little variation with forty-three days under the Bodhi Tree. In India, forty days is the universal time period for a classically structured spiritual discipline.

The "meeting of the day and the night"—or twilight at dawn and dusk, called the *Sandhya* in Sanskrit —is a time of concentrated spiritual power, according to Eastern scriptures. These texts teach that disciplines done in the early morning or at sunset should be more powerful. But dedication and regularity are great powers as well, and I would suggest that it is most important for you to perform your mantra practice at the same time every day, whenever it is most convenient for you. One consideration is that you will find that your ability to concentrate in your practice will usually be better before a meal than after. You can decide to chant once a day or twice a day, according to your schedule.

Practice in the same place if you are able. The vibrations in your meditation spot will grow in power over time. Some people like a bright, sunny room, while others prefer the dark, with shades drawn. Constructing an altar in your meditation place is optional. For many people, an altar is wonderful tool for concentrating the mind and sharpening the focus of meditation. You may or may not use incense, as you prefer. Yoga postures can help focus the mind for meditation, but you should be sure that you are sitting comfortably so that you are not distracted from your practice.

Finally, turn off the phone, close the door if possible, and leave instruction that you are not to be disturbed unless there is some great emergency. This is your personal time. Almost every issue or problem can wait another twenty minutes.

THE MALA

In most cases, a *mala* (a Hindu or Buddhist rosary) is used for keeping count of the number of repetitions. A standard mala has 108 beads, with a *meru* (Sanskrit for "mountain") bead secured separately from the rest. The meru is said to store the power of all of your recitations. After much use, the power in the meru is reputed to have the ability to transmit power from the chanter to a recipient for healing purposes.

During one's practice, recitation is conducted using one bead for each time the mantra is chanted, and then the next bead is used for the next repetition, until the complete circuit of 108 is finished. Since malas usually come in lengths of fifty-four (a half mala) or 108 (a full mala), keeping track of the 108 repetitions is easy enough. Interestingly, the Catholic rosary is also fifty-four beads in length, and the Christian Mystery School in Alexandria calls their prayer beads a mala, not a rosary.

The position of the fingers is also important in mantra practice. Using the right hand, the mala is draped over the middle finger, ring finger, and little finger, with the thumb and first finger free. With the first finger extended, the first mantra is chanted

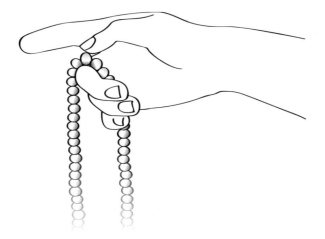

on the first bead south of the meru with the thumb touching the bead. Then the thumb pushes the mala away so that the second bead comes to rest on the thumb, where the next mantra is chanted. This practice continues until all of the beads in the mala have come under the thumb and you return to the meru. The meru is never crossed by the thumb. Instead, if you desire to continue with the repetitions of your mantra, the thumb begins to pull the beads back one at a time with each repetition of your mantra. In this manner, the chanting goes round the mala to the meru, then back again the other way, until the meru is reached again. When the meru is reached again, if you want to continue with your mantra meditation, you begin to return back the other way, and the process repeats itself.

Symbolically, the three fingers involved in moving around the mala are considered to represent the three qualities of nature Positive, Negative, and Neutral. The first finger represents the ego and at no time is it to work with or touch the mala. The thumb represents God or the divine, which is why it is the only digit that moves the mala.

After the mantra practice, the mala is put back in a special place or worn around the neck. The mala increases in spiritual potency with use, and for that reason many people choose to carry it with them. Some people like to wear a mala so that the Meru is positioned at the back of the skull because they feel that the energy radiates into their brain. Others prefer to wear the mala so that the meru sits over the heart, radiating its vibrations there.

One may decide on a certain number of repetitions per day for the forty-day course of the practice. One full mala, or 108 repetitions, is usually the smallest number chanted per day for any discipline. If you have decided to practice one mala per day, it will take only a small amount of time to complete your practice. With some of the shorter mantras, it can take as few as five minutes to complete a mala. In certain situations, such as in the case of the Mantra Siddhi practice explained later, you may choose to do more than one full mala in every sitting. If you chant one mala per day for forty days, you will complete 4,320 repetitions. If you chant two malas, the number for the discipline doubles to 8,640, and so forth.

Why 108 repetitions? It is taught that the *Sacred Heart*, the *Hrit Padma* (the Sanskrit term for the heart chakra), is the location of the soul, the self, *atman*, or the piece of divinity within us that goes by many names. From this chakra, 108 channels, called *Nadis*, radiate out to all parts of the subtle body. These are the equivalent to the system of veins and arteries that circulate the blood through our body. By chanting the mantra 108 times, the energy of the mantra enters each of those channels so that it reaches all parts of the subtle body.

COMMON PROBLEMS OCCURRING DURING MANTRA MEDITATION PRACTICE

I have heard the most amazing stories over the years from people who have tried to reduce various karmic conditions, only to find themselves in the midst of battle, as it were. Usually this barrier appears at any time after the thirtieth day. It may be some family crisis which demands that you completely change your schedule, or you might have to leave town for business, or to deal with some personal matter with relatives. You could get a bad cold or the flu, or something else that interrupts your routine.

These kinds of incidents are very common. They mean that your discipline is working. At some level, the karmic baggage you are attempting to neutralize or dislodge is actually defending itself, and does not want to leave. If your discipline is interrupted, then this karmic material is safe until you begin your forty-day practice again.

This idea of our karma defending itself sounds crazy unless you have tried to quit smoking, or lose weight, or get over a bad relationship. In each case, we feel the lure of the old, accepted behaviors that we began our practice to get away from. In this way, the patterns we have created and reinforced over years or even decades actively resist the change we are trying to make. So, if you find that a whirlwind arises that threatens your practice near the end of a discipline, know that this is evidence that the process is working—you are actually creating real and lasting change in your life.

I am often asked, "What if I miss a day in my practice? Can I just add another day at the end?" Sorry, it is not so simple. If you do, by some misfortune, miss a day, your mantra practice will have effectively ended. I define a day as the time you get up until the time you actually fall asleep at night. So, if you are lying in bed without having fallen asleep, and think, "Oh my God! I didn't do my practice!" you are okay. Get up and do your practice without penalty. But if you fall asleep, even for just a few minutes, too bad. That piece of karma you were trying to dislodge has won a temporary victory, and you must begin your practice over from the very beginning. If you miss a day, you have lost the battle, but not the war. Start again with firm resolve.

If you break your mala and need to restring it, you should chant a couple of rounds of *Hrim* over it before starting or continuing with your spiritual discipline. Since the seed sound for the Hrit Padma or Sacred Heart chakra is *Hrim*, this practice will purify the mala, and "attune" it to you own vibration in your personal Hrit Padma.

If you decide during a discipline that you have changed your mind about that for which you are performing the discipline, just stop. Say a short prayer of gratitude for the insight, and start formulating in your mind what you really do want. Wait four or five days, and then begin your new discipline.

MANTRA SIDDHI

There is also a state one may attain after extensive practice, where the power of the mantra becomes "seated" within you. This state is known as *Mantra Siddhi*, in which one carries the power of the mantra with them into any and all situations. The first, or lowest level of Mantra Siddhi is generally recognized to be achieved with 125,000 repetitions. With Mantra Siddhi, it is not forty days of repetition that matters, but simply the total number of repetitions you achieve or complete. The person who has achieved Mantra Siddhi becomes a bulb shining with the vibration of that mantra. Higher levels of Mantra Siddhi produce the kinds of spiritual abilities detailed in the great spiritual text known as *The Yoga Sutras of Patanjali.*

The greater the attainment of Mantra Siddhi, the more intense the vibration radiated into the environment, and the wider the field of effect. That is why spiritual teachers like the Dalai Lama have a primary aura field that extends for miles. Traveling by car to attend a program to see him one day, we pulled over a hill, and I felt a wave of his energy from a distance of five to seven miles. I am certain that if I had had more sensitivity, I would have felt his energy from an even farther distance.

Often when a student learns of the more extensive practices taught in mantra meditation, they wonder, if these practices require something in excess of 125,000 repetitions, then what kind of results can they expect with the 4,320 repetitions involved in regular mantra practice? The answer is that there is a big difference between working on a problem or attaining a goal, and achieving some of the more elevated states, such as Mantra Siddhi.

It is also true that the more repetitions one focuses on a problem or a goal, the more noticeable or dramatic the result will be. If your karmic predicament is particularly severe, you may not get appreciable results until you have completed 250,000 repetitions or more. It is also possible to obtain results very quickly if your karmic predicament is not so great.

PURASCHARANA

There is a practice called a *Purascharana*, whereby one undertakes to repeat the mantra 100,000 times for each syllable in the mantra. For a simple mantra like *Om*, 100,000 repetitions is relatively simple. *Om Namah Shivaya*, with its six syllables, would require 600,000 repetitions to complete a Purascharana. The long form of the Gayatri Mantra, with its approximately forty-two syllables, would require a bold undertaking of 4,200,000 repetitions to finish the Purascharana.

During the conduct of a Purascharana, daily activities are structured tightly, schedules are devised, and diet is kept pure and simple. Rest is moderated so that it is not too much or too little. This is why a classical Purascharana is rarely observed in the Western world today. Even in India, it is mostly observed only in monasteries and ashrams, but there is no reason why you could not attempt one if that is what you really desire.

Mahatma Gandhi used to say that his life was an experiment with truth. Conduct your own experiments.

CHOOSING GOALS FOR YOUR SADHANA

We all have many desires. Some we can fulfill through the normal means available, working toward the objective. Other objectives seem to continually elude us because we either do not know the correct path to follow for fulfillment, or the desire seems completely out of reach. This problem is very common even in mantra practice when we focus on more than one goal at a time. It is obvious that the more focus you can bring to bear on a single objective, the greater your chances of a significant outcome. Mental focus and heartfelt devotion greatly amplify the power of the mantra, and if you have a long list (or even a short one), the acrobatics of diffused concentration will dilute your results. This means that significant change will be difficult, if not impossible, to accomplish.

Therefore, I always strongly recommend one and only one objective for anyone's first foray into a mantra discipline. This will allow you to focus the power in a single-minded way that connects your mind, your heart, and the sacred sound. After the completion of your first discipline, you can do whatever you want, but I would remind everyone that multiple objectives in your meditation practice will probably dilute your efforts.

What Do You Really Want?

In my book *Healing Mantras,* I describe the efforts of two different women to attract a suitable man. They each independently undertook chanting a mantra designed to bring a spiritually based relationship with a man into a woman's life, and each chanted this mantra for a little over two weeks. Then they both decided to stop the practice.

The first woman told me that she had decided to stop the practice because she had only attracted "bozos." I questioned whether she desired a truly meaningful relationship because any results after only fourteen days of a forty-day discipline, even if they are not the ones we ultimately desire, should have been encouraging. Even so, she decided to give up her mantra practice.

The second woman, whom I will call Tracy here, also decided that she wanted a spiritual man for a life partner, and chanted the mantra for a couple of weeks, then stopped, without really knowing why. Six months went by, and then she decided that she should give her mantra practice another try. Again, she lasted about two weeks and then stopped. Another several months went by, and then one morning she was struck with the question, "Did I really want to find a good man with whom a solid relationship was probable, or didn't I?" She sat down and examined her motives and her desires and tried to get at her innermost thoughts and feelings on the matter. She decided that she really did want such a relationship, so she began the discipline again with the combined powers of her heart and mind and focus. This time, she completed the forty-day mantra discipline and called to tell me that within five days of its competition, she had met her soul mate while riding on a bus.

There is an obvious lesson here for all of us: Before we decide that any practice in our life is failing to bring us the result we want, we should first examine very deeply if what we think we want is what we really want with all our heart and soul. This process of self-inquiry can be as enriching as any mantra discipline, and it is necessary for anything in our lives—including our meditation practice—to be truly successful.

A NOTE ON THE HINDU PANTHEON OF GODS AND GODDESSES

One of the most misunderstood aspects of classical Hinduism is the pantheon of gods and goddesses. Because there are a variety of "deities," many people assume that Hinduism is polytheistic, but this is not really true. When we examine the saints of the Roman Catholic Church, we understand that just because there are many saints does not mean that Catholicism is polytheistic. Hinduism is best understood in the same light.

Each of the gods and goddesses in Hinduism represents a specific principle of a monotheistic divinity. Some people believe that these beings have actually existed in animal or human form at one time, and are now liberated souls who have returned to help us on our paths. Others believe that the principles represented have been anthropomorphized into "characters" so that the concepts behind the principles may be more easily understood. It is certainly easier to tell a story than it is to dryly explain a principle.

For the purposes of this program, it does not matter which of these scenarios you believe. It is enough to understand that an ancient system of understanding the principles that underlie our life and experience has formed and been transmitted through thousands of years of oral and written tradition, using these individual gods and goddesses to represent aspects of spiritual power and ability. The qualities embodied by each individual member of the pantheon can then be used as a table of organization of the divine abilities available to you.

Some of the anthropomorphized principles featured in the following mantras include:

Ganesha (also called *Ganapati*) is the remover of obstacles. He accomplishes this by unifying disparate parts of our selves until everything is under the direction of the mind and will. This state is often called *Cosmic Consciousness*, for which Ganesha/Ganapati is the presiding deity.

Lakshmi is a member of the Hindu feminine trinity, and the feminine power of any kind of abundance. She can provide food, children, a new job, and prosperity. She also has a higher form of activity that one might call *manifestation*, through transcendental shakti, as described in the Hindu scripture *The Laksmi Tantra*.

Vishnu is the member of the masculine trinity that manifests through gurus, spiritual teachers, adepts, ministers, rabbis, mullahs, or any other living propounder of dharma. Vishnu also sends great beings to the planet, from time to time, to help humanity's evolution as a species. These are called the *Avatars of Vishnu*, the most recent of which was the Buddha.

Shiva is the member of the Hindu masculine trinity who represents the all-pervading consciousness that exists in everything. To be able to unify and work with consciousness at all levels of creation is to become a *Siddha*, or perfected being.

Chamundi is the great feminine force for good, for protection of virtue and divine law (dharma), who cannot be defeated by any negative force whatsoever. She is an emanation of *Durga*, a member of the Hindu feminine trinity.

CHAPTER
SIX

Mantras for Artha, or Abundance

WHEN FRED (not his real name) called from Chicago several years ago, he told me an amazing story. He had been having problems with his business and, while reading *Healing Mantras*, he was moved to undertake a Lakshmi Mantra discipline using *Om Shrim Maha Lakshmiyei Swaha*. Deciding against a standard forty-day approach, he instead opted for the more difficult attainment of the first phase of Mantra Siddhi, which means that he would have to complete 125,000 repetitions.

Fred was disciplined and dedicated, and completed the first phase of Mantra Siddhi in about three months. Still he did not attain the changes in his business that had led him to begin his mantra practice. Undaunted, he decided to do another discipline identical to the first one. He plunged into his practice and completed the next 125,000 in a little over three months. Still nothing had changed.

But Fred was undaunted. He did not blame the mantra for the lack of result, and he did not blame me. Instead he reasoned that millions of people had experienced great results using this spiritual formula over the hundreds and hundreds of years it had been available, so the fault must reside in his "karmic predicament." He decided to try one more time.

Again he performed the arduous discipline to attain Mantra Siddhi, and in a little over four months he reached 125,000 repetitions for the third time, for a total of 375,000. This time, the floodgates of prosperity opened to his business. Only then did he pick up the phone to tell me what had happened.

Well-known author and spiritual teacher Iyanla Vanzant had a completely different karmic experience. She has studied and integrated Sanskrit mantra work as part of the great fund of spiritual knowledge at her disposal. When I returned from one of my frequent road trips giving workshops, I had an amazing message from Iyanla on my answering machine: "I have been traveling and wanted to give my staff a discipline to do while I was gone. I asked them to gather every morning just before lunch and do at least 108 repetitions of the mantra, *Om Shrim Maha Lakshmiyei Swaha*. They did it for the two weeks I was away, and when I returned, there was a message from the publisher of my first book. A routine audit had revealed that there had been an error in the money they had sent to me. They were now sending me a check for $125,000 with their apologies for the error."

There is an obvious lesson here. None of us really knows the extent of our karma in any area of our life, and spiritual disciplines employed to solve problems will have different results based upon our karma. Sometimes, like Fred, we intuitively know that this is the case, and endeavor to take on a more strenuous mantra practice from the first. And sometimes, even when it does not at first appear to be working, we decide not to abandon the practice, but rather to continue until we get the results that we want.

It is difficult for us to know why the same practices give different results to different people, but many of us who know Iyanla know that, although her life has not always been easy, she is an embodiment of the positive values and faith that have inspired hundreds of thousands of people through her books and public appearances. And, obviously, her karma with money and abundance issues is much, much different from Fred's.

THE ESOTERIC LAKSHMI MANTRA

LISTEN TO TRACK 1
The Esoteric Lakshmi Mantra

Om Gum Shrim Maha Lakshmiyei Swaha

Let all obstacles to my abundance be eliminated and the flow of the shakti of abundance released within me.

Goal Today, I would recommend this mantra, instead of the Lakshmi Mantra discipline, to Fred after quizzing him about his previous attempts to achieve abundance. His karmic burden appears to have been especially difficult, and the addition of the *gum* syllable would have helped him overcome that karma. This mantra was taught by my teacher and guru, Sadguru Sant Keshavadas, and does not yet appear in any of the popular or specialized books on mantra printed in English and published in the United States.

Use this mantra for embedded karmic obstacles specifically related to abundance.

If you feel, from your life experience, that you have particularly difficult karma surrounding finances or the attracting of prosperity, then this mantra is especially useful in working through the karma involved. For the majority of people seeking to improve their financial picture, the *Om Shrim Maha Lakshmiyei Swaha* mantra will work very well. But if you know from experience that every attempt at increasing your prosperity has not worked well, then add the *Gum* seed sound as indicated above.

The Elements of the Mantra

Om Like the great majority of all mantras, this Lakshmi mantra begins with *Om*, because it is the seed sound for the sixth (*Ajna*) chakra, which is located in the center of the forehead, about a half-inch above the line of the eyebrows, sometimes referred to as the mystic "third eye." From here, the principle of mind directs all that follows in the rest of the mantra.

Gum The next syllable is *Gum*, which is the seed sound for Ganapati, a form of Ganesha, the Hindu God known as the remover of obstacles, who is often portrayed in the form of an elephant.

Shrim The application of that obstacle-removing sound is then qualified by Lakshmi's seed sound *Shrim*, which refers to abundance of all kinds.

Maha A salutation that means both "great" and "heart-centered."

Lakshmi Refers to the feminine principle.

Yei A shakti-activating sound.

Swaha A traditional ending of mantras, where its meaning is "I salute and by so doing I automatically invoke her power."

THE MANTRA OF KUBERA, THE CELESTIAL GUARDIAN OF RICHES

LISTEN TO TRACK 2
The Mantra of Kubera

Ha Sa Ka La E I La Hrim

Ha Sa Ka La E I La Hrim

There is no translation possible of this mantra, since it is composed solely of seed syllables.

Goal Use this mantra to attain great wealth that, once achieved, will be self-sustaining.

This is particularly true if you are in an occupation where you safeguard money or investments for others. *Kubera* is often referred to as the celestial who is the Divine Treasurer. So if you are an investment counselor, stock broker, real estate broker, or work in some similar capacity, this mantra will greatly aid in the discharging of your financial responsibilities while also providing you with abundance.

Elements of the Mantra

Note: Observe that the same set of sounds is repeated twice in this mantra.

Ha Sa Although this mantra begins with *Ha* and *Sa* instead of *Om*, these sounds are also designed to bring energy to the Ajna chakra.

Ka La This brings the energy of the Ajna chakra into connection with the *Kala* (Ka La) chakra, literally the wheel of time, located in the upper chest between the heart center and the throat center.

E The letter E (pronounced e-e-e-e) sends energy from the *medulla oblongata* (located at the base of the skull) down the back side of the spine to the *Muladhara* (first) chakra, at the base of the spine.

I This is really the sounds *Ah* and *E. Ah* resounds in the upper chest, and *E* works again as discussed earlier.

La This is the seed sound of the first chakra (*Lam*) with the *m* left off. This means that the sound *La* is voiced, but the vibration is just short of actual anchoring on the Earth Plane since it is the voiced m on the end of any seed sound that would anchor it here on the Earth Plane.

Hrim This is the seed sound of the esoteric *Hrit Padma* (also called the *Hridayam* in some texts) located two fingers below the *Anahata* chakra, which corresponds to the heart center in the physical body.

The Story of Kubera

In a past epoch described in the scriptures and stories of India, the *Asuras*—or the negative forces in the universe—fought the celestials in an attempt to overthrow them and take over their positions. First they knew they had to defeat Indra, the chief of the celestials who led the armies of the positive forces against them. But perhaps there was none of the celestials whose power they wanted more than Kubera's, who was the custodian and guardian of Divine Wealth in the form of gold, silver, and precious gems. If the Asuras were to wage war on the celestials, they knew that they needed Kubera's wealth.

Kubera was originally one of the negative forces, but when his glistening fortress on the water in Sri Lanka was stolen by the demon leader Ravana, Kubera fled to the northern part of India, and undertook a strenuous spiritual practice that garnered the attention and blessing of Brahma. Due to his extraordinary penance and discipline, Kubera was converted to the positive forces in the universe, and granted the status of an immortal, and appointed guardian of the North and custodian of Divine Wealth. Thus, Kubera's mantra brings great wealth to the chanter.

The purpose of this mantra is to invoke the natural wealth of the universe, always available through the chakras, and send it down to the Earth Plane. It is important to keep in mind that the individual soul, located in the Hrit Padma, must agree to the manner of dispensing the wealth. That is why we respectfully omit the *m* of the seed sound *Lam* and by ending the mantra with the salutation *Hrim* directed to the Hrit Padma.

It is always advisable to offer a short, mental salutation to Kubera before beginning a dedicated discipline with this mantra. Simply silently offer, "Salutations to Kubera, the Divine Treasurer." Alternatively, one might chant, "Om Kuberaya Namaha."

CHAPTER
SEVEN

Mantras for Kama, or Fulfillment of Desires

WE HAVE SO MANY desires that it would be hard to catalog them all. We might believe that we have only a few desires until situations come up that we do not care for, and then we will discover that we have even more desires than we realized. Even as some desires are met or satisfied, others take their place. This is a natural, normal part of the human existence.

There is nothing wrong with having desires. I say this because so many spiritual paths centered on Eastern practices teach that desires are bad or that you should stop having desires. To my way of thinking, you can no more stop the process of desiring than you can stop the process of breathing. The inner push toward enlightenment or to achieve Moksha (spiritual freedom) is a desire. Even teachings that warn against desires attempt to get us to desire a life without desires.

My teacher, Sadguru Sant Keshavadas, used to teach that desires are part of the human condition. The trick is to substitute desires that lead to greater fulfillment for ones that do not help us. Eventually, with dedicated spiritual discipline, we will naturally arrive at a spiritual condition where certain desires effortlessly fall away. We no longer desire the same things we did when we were children, not because we decided that those desires were bad for us, but because in the natural process of growing older they no longer satisfied us. They fell away naturally and were replaced by other, wiser, or more mature desires. So cultivate healthy desires and use them to replace negative desires, and use these good desires to gradually advance to a place where you can naturally pass into a desireless state without effort. As one of the great Eastern maxims says, "You cannot rip the skin from the snake, it must shed it of itself."

There are times when your sincerity alone takes you over and through a nest of karmic scorpions. Sincerity attracts the assistance of the masters and gurus to move us to the next spiritual state. Sincerity also invokes Grace. But if we try to fool ourselves into believing that what we desire will be good for us when we know in our hearts that it is not, not only will we lose divine assistance, but we will also betray ourselves and what is in our best interests. Ultimately, we can never fool anyone for very long, least of all ourselves.

A SHIVA MANTRA FOR FULFILLMENT OF DESIRES

LISTEN TO TRACK 3
A Shiva Mantra

Om Sarva Kamadaya Namaha
Salutations to the granter of desires.

Goal Use this short mantra to petition the Great Consciousness to fulfill your individual desires. Every desire is tied to our consciousness. This mantra attracts the elements of universal consciousness that fulfill desires strongly held by the mind.

Elements of the Mantra
Om The seed sound for the sixth (Ajna) chakra, from which the principle of mind directs all that follows.
Sarva "Source of."
Kamadaya That which grants fulfillment of desires.
Namaha "I invoke by saluting."

This is a Shiva mantra because it is addressed to Shakti, or the primal energy of Shiva that rises out of the wellspring of compassion, and thus is automatically part of sentient self-consciousness existing everywhere in the universe.

Sarva can mean "source of." Used here, the implication is that desires are part of the nature of universal consciousness and naturally arise in individual consciousness. In fact, the tales and parables concerning Shiva invariably show him absorbed in contemplating his own nature, just as we are completely consumed with the details of our own lives. Only when one merges into universal truth so completely that individual existence ceases altogether does desire in our normal understanding of the word cease.

You can chant this mantra for the fulfillment of individual desires, but do not make a long list of desires before you begin to chant. Instead, focus your attention and concentrate your will in order to select an individual desire to be fulfilled. Once you have selected a specific goal, you can begin your mantra practice.

A GANESHA/GANAPATI MANTRA

Shrim Hrim Klim

Glaum Gum Ganapatayei

Sarva Janam Me

Vasha-manaya Swaha

LISTEN TO TRACK 4
A Ganesha/Ganapati Mantra

Since there are so many seed sounds in this mantra, it is essentially untranslatable. However, the sense of it is that we are asking that obstacles and difficulties be dissolved back into their source and that the energy be returned to us in usable form.

Goal Use this mantra for the removal of those things (known and unknown) that may stand in the way of fulfilling a specific desire. Few of us have control over the circumstances of our lives. This mantra is a fusion of the principles of consciousness and energy so that, blossoming in your mind and consciousness, they will reveal how to actively work with the conditions in which you find yourself, whatever they are. Sometimes the mechanism is through a proper understanding that indicates a course of action, or sometimes it is through some application of pressure or energy to a given situation. It varies from one instance to another.

Selected Elements of the Mantra

Shrim Hrim Notice that the seed sound for abundance is the very first mantra sound (*Shrim*), followed by the seed sound for the Hrit Padma (*Hrim*), both already discussed.

Klim The seed sound for attraction. It concentrates and attracts those things that surround it.

Glaum Removes obstacles between the root (base of the spine) and the throat (power of Will through the spoken word).

Gum The seed sound for removing obstacles of any kind, known or unknown.

Sarva "Source of."

Swaha A traditional ending of mantras, where its meaning is "I salute, and by so doing I automatically invoke her power."

Sometimes the obstacles we have created in other lifetimes are very difficult to surmount. In such cases, some form of the Maha Ganapati Mantra can be very useful. The Maha Ganapati Mantra is actually a series of mantras that rise in length and complexity like steps. I write more about these mantras in Volume I of my three-volume work *The Ancient Power of Sanskrit Mantra and Ceremony*. Here is a medium-sized form of the mantra that asks that Ganapati remove the very source of the obstacle.

THE AHAM PREMA MANTRA

Aham Prema

LISTEN TO TRACK 5
Aham Prema Mantra

I am Divine Love

Goal Use this mantra to attract a spiritually based relationship.

The mantra *Aham Prema* declares that one's nature is composed of Divine Love. To chant this mantra is to ground your search for a spiritually-based relationship in your own ultimate nature, thus attracting others who are looking for the same kind of relationship, based on a similar identification with their own ultimate nature.

Elements of the Mantra

Aham "I am."

Prema Divine Love.

THE DHANVANTRE MANTRA

Om Shri Dhanvantre Namaha

LISTEN TO TRACK 6
The Dhanvantre Mantra

Om and Salutations to the Celestial Healer

Goal Use this mantra to find the best resolution for a medical problem.

One of the tasks we all face when a health problem arises is finding an appropriate physician or practitioner for our problem among so many choices. In Hinduism, the celestial healer or physician is known as *Dhanvantre*, and his mantra is chanted when one is looking for guidance to find the most appropriate path to healing.

Elements of the Mantra

Om The seed sound for the sixth (Ajna) chakra, from which the principle of mind directs all that follows.

Shri Invoking the power of Lakshmi, the transcendental power of manifestation.

Dhanvantre The celestial healer.

Namaha "I invoke by saluting."

CHAPTER
EIGHT

Mantras for Upholding Dharma

THE TERM *DHARMA* has a wide application, ranging from spiritual law to ethical and moral behavior. Here, I mean a little of both. By performing your ethical and moral duties in this life and by supporting spiritual law, you are automatically following your *swadharma*, or the law of your own life. The fact that you are reading this book means that, at some level, you are already a supporter of dharma, or you would not be attracted to it at all.

There are mantras that will help you to lead a life that is in tune with the "inner you." Through this attunement, you will naturally manifest spiritual law aligned with proper ethics, as well as maintaining moral behavior and outlook.

PROTECTION AGAINST NEGATIVE FORCES—THE STORY OF CHAMUNDI

Although many people in the West are familiar with Kali, the primal feminine goddess in classical Hinduism, very few have heard the ancient tale of Chamundi, which is found in the *Devi Mahatmyam*, the final portion of the *Markandeya Purana*.

Just before the creation of our cosmos, at the time of the birth of Brahma, two demonic entities were created who desired to wreak havoc on Brahma. They started to swim through the inky void toward where he was being born, but Brahma was under the protection of the Great Feminine in the form of Lakshmi. She banished the two troublemakers to the farthest reaches of the newly forming reality (the universe) which was about to be created, believing that it would take a long, long time before they could make their way back to cause more problems.

One day, long after the creation of our cosmos, these demonic entities returned from the farthest reaches of reality to cause problems. Representing the polar opposites of good and noble qualities, these demons are often seen as the antithesis of spiritual growth and progress. Since we know that this universe is composed of pairs of opposites (good and evil, positive and negative, and so on), these negative entities are actually part of the engine that makes our reality function, and their ultimate absorption into the fabric of spiritual evolution is part of our personal and cosmic evolution.

Since these entities possessed incredible power, they defeated the celestials (or the noble and good qualities of conscious existence), who were then forced to scatter and hide in various planes of existence. Seeking assistance from Indra, chief of the celestials, and Vishnu, the compassionate savior of conscious entities, the celestials were finally directed to Shiva, who advised them to invoke the Great Feminine through a fire ceremony as prescribed by scripture.

As they performed the ceremony, a portion of shakti emanated from each of the gathered celestials and swirled over the fire, taking the form of a feminine figure, Chamundi, riding a lion. She spoke to them. "Even though I am composed from all of you, I am beholden to none of you. I am not your spouse or your personal shakti. I am not a consort to any one of you. I am wholly independent. However, since I come from all of you, I am also aware of your difficulty, which I will now resolve."

With that, she left and sought out the demonic entities and their huge armies to engage them in battle. She prevailed, of course, and the celestials sang her praises, which pleased her enough that she promised to return at any time that evil threatened humankind if her praises were sung and her mantras chanted.

THE GREAT MANTRA OF CHAMUNDI

LISTEN TO TRACK 7
The Great Mantra of Chamundi

Om Eim Hrim Klim Chamundayei Vicche Namah
Salutations to She who is always victorious.

Goal Use this mantra as a means of protection against negative forces. Invoking the power of knowledge through *Eim*, a proactive protecting energy is generated from the shakti at the base of the spine, that is able to work with the shakti that permeates everything. Such a force, directed by universal intelligence, is irresistible. An amazing fringe benefit of this mantra that has been reported to me by many people is that it conveys a sense of self-confidence in the chanter, particularly if the chanter is female.

Elements of the Mantra

Om The seed sound for the sixth (Ajna) chakra, from which the principle of mind directs all that follows.

Eim The seed sound for Saraswati, the goddess who presides over knowledge, the arts and sciences, and the power of speech.

Hrim The seed sound for the *Hrit Madma*, located just below the Anahata chakra in the area of the heart.

Klim The seed sound for the principle of attraction.

Chamundi The feminine force.

Yei A shakti-activating sound.

Vicche Thought by some scholars and organizations to be a form of *Vijay*, which means victory.

Namaha "I invoke by saluting."

THE GAYATRI MANTRA

Om Bhu Om Bhuvaha Om Swaha

Om Maha Om Janaha Om Tapaha Om Satyam

Om Tat Savitur Varenyam

Bhargo Devasya Dhimahi

Dhiyo Yonaha Prachodayat

O Self-Effulgent Light that has given birth to all the lokas (spheres of consciousness), who is worthy of worship and appears through the orbit of the Sun, illumine our intellect.

LISTEN TO TRACK 8

The Gayatri Mantra

Goal Use this mantra to illuminate your intellect. Saying this mantra automatically supports dharma in the world as well as your individual *swadharma*, a word that refers to the law of your own being or nature. As this mantra is chanted over time, spiritual light is drawn into each chakra, starting at the base of the spine. Correspondingly, our ability to comprehend the essence of each of the realms grows. In meditation, travel of consciousness to the higher realms becomes possible as new faculties of consciousness grow from our practice.

Elements of the Mantra

The Gayatri Mantra is a universe in miniature through the power of sound.

Om Bhur Om and Salutations to the Earth Plane (1st chakra).

Om Bhuvaha Om and Salutations to the Atmospheric Plane (2nd chakra).

Om Swaha Om and Salutations to the Solar Region (3rd chakra).

Om Maha Om and Salutations to the First Spiritual Region Beyond the Sun (4th chakra).

Om Janaha Om and Salutations to the Second Spiritual Region Beyond the Sun (5th chakra).

Om Tapaha Om and Salutations to the Third Spiritual Region Beyond the Sun, Sphere of the progenitors (6th chakra).

Om Satyam Om and Salutations to the The Abode of Supreme Truth (7th chakra).

Om Tat Savitur Varenyam Om and Salutations to that realm which is beyond human comprehension.

Bhargo Devasya Dhimahi In that place where all the celestials of all the spheres have ...

Dhiyo Yonaha Prachodayat Received enlightenment, kindly enlighten our intellect.

There is more to upholding dharma than just combating evil. The *I Ching* states that the best way to conquer evil is to make energetic progress toward the good. One of the most effective ways to make progress toward the good is to actively seek enlightenment.

The Gayatri Mantra appears in the *Rig Veda* in a form of twenty-four Sanskrit syllables. For this reason, it is widely practiced in India in this form. However, the complete form of the mantra that was given to the Sage Vishwamitra, who is the seer of the mantra, is a bit longer.

The Gayatri Mantra is said to contain all powers of all mantras, and is also known as the source of all knowledge and the "Mother of the Vedas," but its primary application is for illumination of the intellect. An illumined intellect can contain immeasurable knowledge, including a complete understanding of what we call "power." Those who have attained the full fruit of this mantra are in the company of the highest beings in the universe.

THE GREAT MANI MANTRA

LISTEN TO TRACK 9
The Great Mani Mantra

Om Mani Padme Hum
The Jewel of consciousness has reached the heart's Lotus.

Goal Use this mantra to unite heart and mind. The circulation of energy through the centers listed below builds links among mind, will, and heart. There is a saying in the East, "When the light of the heart is united with power of the mind, anything is possible."

Elements of the Mantra

Om Activates the Ajna chakra between the eyebrows.
Mani Sends energy to the *Manas* chakra in the back of the head.
Padme In this context, *Padme* sends energy to the Anahata chakra at the heart.
Hum A seed sound that activates the *Vishuddha* chakra at the throat.

The Great Mani Mantra is the most often chanted mantra in the world. Pulling energy from the lower chakras into the upper ones, it activates these centers and circulates energy around them, magnetizing the upper spine so that the energy in the subtle body becomes centered in the upper part of the body. The heart and mental chakras become predominant, leading to the ability to exist as a conscious entity without a physical body. As with the Gayatri Mantra, when this mantra is chanted by anyone, all of humanity is benefited.

THE DATTATREYA MANTRA

LISTEN TO TRACK 10
The Dattatreya Mantra

Om Dram Om Guru Dattaya Namaha
Salutations to the Eternal Enlightener of souls.

Goal Use this mantra to sharpen your skills as a spiritual counselor and teacher, as well as moving your personal dharma forward. Dattatreya is the first *guru*, so named in the records from India. There were always teachers and sages, but he was the first being charged with the responsibility of leading souls back to their ever-conscious divinity. This mantra invokes his energy into your life and activities.

Elements of the Mantra

Om The seed sound activating the Ajna chakra at the brow center.

Dram The seed sound for the Guru Principle manifesting in a form, usually meaning a physical body.

Guru The transcendental principle of enlightenment, spiritual instruction, and Grace of God that can manifest at any time, any place, through any thing or entity, physical or non-physical. The operation of this is a true spiritual mystery, and there are no limits placed upon how this principle may manifest.

Dattaya Refers to and invokes the presence of that entity who exists, but without a physical body, who is the primal and first individual guru whose sole purpose was the redemption of souls.

Namaha The energy of salutation that automatically invokes that which precedes it.

The ancient spiritual being Dattatreya, who transmitted spiritual knowledge and eliminated karma for some of his students, is the first known *guru* in the specific application of the word. There were sages (*rishis*) and beings of great knowledge and power (*Maha Siddhas*) who often acted in the role of teacher or spiritual benefactor to students, but Dattatreya was the first recorded being whose primary job was the leading of souls back to their highest divinity. The syllables *Gu* and *Ru* refer to that which dispels the darkness of ignorance, leading to the release of the actual spiritual light within. The nimbus or halo of the saints and sages is a well-known manifestation of this light. But gurus have the responsibility to lead many souls back to their divine birthright, even over many lifetimes.

The Story of How Dattatreya Came into Existence

Among the ten great immortal sages (called the *Prajapati*) is Atri, whose wife, Anasuya, shares his exalted state of consciousness. In the ancient days, all of the highest rishis and sages were householders. Husbands and wives shared a state of consciousness as well as all spiritual knowledge. After years of study and meditation, the highest mysteries of Lakshmi were revealed to Anasuya, and she became contented beyond any human measure.

In this story, the Hindu Masculine Trinity—Brahma, Vishnu, and Shiva—heard about the great knowledge of the cosmos that had come to Anasuya, and they were curious to know if it were really true. Of the three, Vishnu alone knew that her attainment was actual because his spouse, Lakshmi, had herself revealed the mysteries of creation to Anasuya, and this had been made immediately known to Vishnu. Discussing the exalted state of Anasuya's knowledge with their wives (Durga, Saraswati and, of course, Lakshmi) and at their urging, the three gods decided to pay a visit to Anasuya to test her spiritual attainment. Knocking upon her door, they appeared disguised as travelers and begged Anasuya for some food. Anasuya knew well the ancient tradition that a god might arrive at your door as an unknown and unannounced guest, and she invited the three men in.

As she started to leave the room to prepare food for them, one of the three insulted her in the worst way possible by asking that she serve them while naked. Unperturbed for even a moment, Anasuya inquired if that was, indeed, what they desired. They agreed that this was exactly what they desired—she should serve them food while completely undressed.

Anasuya went to a nearby jug of water that she had used to perform a *puja* (religious ceremony) propitiating Lakshmi earlier that day. She returned with a few drops of water in the palm of her hand. Before the gods could analyze what she was doing, Anasuya sprinkled a few drops of water over them while chanting some mantras. Instantly, they were transformed into infants, whereupon she opened her sari and fed each from her breast.

When their husbands failed to return, the Feminine Trinity decided that they should go to the home of Atri and Anasuya to see what had happened. They knocked on the door of Anasuya, who greeted them with reverence. She was about to bow at the feet of Lakshmi, but a glance from the goddess stopped her and conveyed that she should go along with things for the present. Without hinting at the mystical knowledge that Lakshmi had given her, Anasuya invited them in and asked if she could wash their feet as a way of expressing reverence. While the goddesses were pleased at the devotion displayed by Anasuya, they had other pressing matters on their minds, and replied that they might receive such an act later, but for now they were searching for their husbands.

With folded palms, Anasuya explained how three men had come and asked her to serve them food while naked. She also revealed how she had complied with their request by turning them into infants and feeding them from her breast. The goddesses exchanged glances, with only Lakshmi knowing the full extent of the drama. Somewhat nervously, Durga explained that the three travelers were really their husbands, who had come to test Anasuya. They had heard of her spiritual attainment, and wanted to see if it was factual. With all courtesy, Saraswati requested that Anasuya turn the infants back again into their husbands.

With complete devotion, Anasuya replied that since she had no children, she had become fond of the infants. If she turned them back into the travelers that had stopped at her door, all of them would leave, and she would no longer have any children. All that would remain was the hole created by their departure.

Anasuya asked a pointed question, while still remaining respectful and reverent: "Is it right to test one's spiritual attainment and have pain and disappointment be the result, even if all tests were passed effortlessly?" Anasuya noted that she did not seek the travelers, they sought her. She did not seek to test them, but they her. She did not offer to serve them while naked, but it was their own rude request. "Is it right," she asked, "that I now suffer the pangs of separation from those beautiful babies as a reward for passing all tests by none other than the Male Trinity itself?" The Feminine Trinity fell silent with guilt. Except for Lakshmi, they had freely agreed with their husbands that Anasuya should be tested. Now they were reaping the results from their complicity by their separation from their husbands.

After an awkward silence, Lakshmi spoke. "It is true that you have passed every test, including suffering a great insult without inflicting harm in any way. Therefore, tell us what you want to satisfy the indignation you have received through no fault of your own."

Anasuya replied without hesitation, "I have enjoyed having these babies here with me. Please leave one of them here so that I may have a child to raise."

The three goddesses looked at one another trying to construct a graceful way out of the mess in which they now found themselves.

But Lakshmi spoke immediately and relieved the tension in a bold stroke. "We shall do better than that. We will leave a portion of the essence of each of these infants in a single baby boy that you can have to raise as your own. In this way, you will have three babies in one, and we will have our husbands back."

Anasuya smiled with great joy and bowed down reverently before them. "I accept your bounteous gift with gratitude."

Thereupon, the three babies in the next room instantly returned to their previous forms as the masculine trinity. Leaving the bedroom of the small cottage, they emerged with palms folded toward both their wives and Anasuya in a gesture of respect. Vishnu spoke, "You have more than passed the test put to you. We salute your knowledge of the cosmos and the love and reverence with which you wield this knowledge."

Then Vishnu produced a small ball of substance and asked Brahma and Shiva to each place their hands upon it, as he did likewise. Standing with eyes closed in meditative pose for a few seconds, the three simultaneously opened their eyes, and Vishnu handed the ball of substance to Anasuya as he spoke. "This sweet cake contains our vibration in strong measure. Consume it, and you will gain a child of great spiritual stature, whose essence will be one with our own." So saying, the three gods and the three goddesses all joined their palms in salute to Anasuya, and departed.

Anasuya consumed the sweet cake, and soon after came a child from her called Dattatreya. That great spiritual prodigy was destined to become the first guru on the Earth Plane and would be called "the guru of all the gurus."

CHAPTER
NINE

Mantras for Moksha, or Liberation

SPIRITUAL LIBERATION is a bit hard to wrap the mind around. So complete is our freedom when we achieve Moksha that we do not ever have to come back into human embodiment unless we choose to do so. If we decide that the spirit world of plants is more aligned with our current nature, we may instead chose to leave the human life form altogether and work as a sentient spirit being with the plant kingdom on this or other planets. Or we may feel as if we want to become the spirit of an entire planet. For this, we would go to school (in spirit) to learn the details of how to be that spirit with knowledge and purpose. We may also choose to be a part of the Great Work regarding humanity and toil in spirit for human redemption, or return to Earth as a liberated being to help humanity. Achieving Moksha or Mukti is a prerequisite for any of the above choices.

THE VASUDEVA MANTRA

Om Namo Bhagavate Vasudevaya

Om is the name of the In-dweller who is in constant contact with all of creation. Salutations.

LISTEN TO TRACK 11
The Vasudeva Mantra

Goal Use this mantra to obtain spiritual freedom. The essence of the Divine is everywhere, but we identify with our individual ego-centered existence. This mantra builds a link between conscious divinity at every level of creation and our own ego-based consciousness. Eventually, our sense of identity changes to include all life, even as we know we are living in an individual body.

Elements of the Mantra

Om The seed sound for the sixth (Ajna) chakra, from which the principle of mind directs all that follows.

Namo Here means "name of."

Bhagavate Our own completely integrated divine self that we are in the process of becoming.

Vasudevaya The in-dwelling divinity that you are entreating to permeate your mind, personality, ego, and being.

The Sanskrit term *Vasudeva* means "the In-dweller" referring to the soul or atman. Since the soul is always divine and a part of God everywhere, the Vasudeva Mantra, at an advanced level, can be a vehicle for uniting with divinity anywhere in the cosmos.

The mechanics of the mantra are simple: When the twelve syllables are chanted, energy is rotated around the spine, stimulating the positive and negative poles of the chakras. The energy first goes down the spine, then back up. After the mantra is chanted many thousands of times, energy is rotated around the spine to such an extent that it becomes spiritually magnetized. This allows for higher vibrations and octaves of spiritual energy to be invoked and held in the subtle body. Finally, the subtle body becomes so energy-based that it can ultimately survive without its physical counterpart.

The Vasudeva Mantra is the one that *Prahalad*—one of the great child *bhaktas* (those strongly or entirely devoted to God)—was initiated into by the great sage, Narada, while still in the womb. This mantra, practiced by Prahalad as a very young child, led to his complete spiritual freedom.

TARAKA RAMA MANTRA

Om Sri Rama Jay Rama Jaya Jaya Rama

Om and victory to Rama and Sita, victory to Rama again and again.

LISTEN TO TRACK 12
Taraka Rama Mantra

Goal Use this mantra to begin the process of purification of the ego and personality that will eventually lead to spiritual freedom. In this mantra, *Rama* is the divine self within. All difficulties and problems—including eradication of karma itself—can be solved if we allow the divinity within to handle everything. This is the "victory" of the self within that is indicated in the translation.

Elements of the Mantra

Om The seed sound for the sixth (Ajna) chakra, from which the principle of mind directs all that follows.

Sri Refers to the all-powerful energy of Sita.

Rama The syllables *Ra* and *Ma* balance energy in the masculine and feminine channels in the body, located on the right and left sides of the body, respectively. As Rama, it also refers to the avatar himself, as well as to the divine self within.

Jaya Means "victory."

Taraka means that which "takes one across." In this case, the "across" refers to the ocean of rebirth, this *samsara* that keeps us coming back again and again to assume bodies and burn off, as well as accumulate, karma. This mantra, practiced by Mahatma Gandhi from the time he was a young boy, will free one from the round of rebirth. Gandhi was heard to say "Hey Ram" at the time of his death, when he was pierced by an assassin's bullet. In *The Ramayana*, the epic story of the life of Sita and Rama (the seventh Avatar of Vishnu), this and other mantras pertaining to Sita and Rama are given. However, this particular mantra is uniformly recommended for transcending karma.

PARAMESHWARI MANTRA

Hrim Shrim Klim Param Eshwari Swaha

Salutations to the Supreme Feminine. May that abundant principle that hides the nature of ultimate reality be attracted to me, and reveal the true nature of reality to me.

LISTEN TO TRACK 13
Parameshwari Mantra

Goal Use this mantra to activate shakti to master the elements of nature in your life. Just as the Siddha Mantra *Om Namah Shivaya* can transform one to become a perfected being, this mantra achieves the same state by a different route. Merely by saying the mantra one achieves ever-unfolding mastery over the elements composing *The Matrika*—the Great Feminine.

Elements of the Mantra

Hrim The seed sound for the Hrit Padma.

Shrim The seed sound for abundance.

Klim The seed sound for attraction. It concentrates and attracts those things that surround it.

Param Supreme.

Eshwari The feminine principle.

Swaha "I salute and, by so doing, I automatically invoke."

The sense of this mantra is that by propitiating shakti as the Great Feminine both within and without, we awaken our individual shakti so that it moves progressively up the spine, activating each of the chakras in new and powerful ways, eventually arriving at the *Sahasrara* chakra at the top of the head. Here one has become Shiva and is automatically a Siddha.

The Kula sect in Kashmir has, for centuries, worshipped *Shiva* (consciousness) by a different route. Although many of their practices are shrouded in mystery, it is common knowledge that they state openly that, since Shakti is the power of Shiva, it is She who brings one into union with Shiva, or to literally become Shiva. Since She makes one Shiva, then it stands to reason that the Great Feminine should be propitiated to become a Siddha.

THE ENHANCED SIDDHA MANTRA

LISTEN TO TRACK 14
The Enhanced Siddha Mantra

Om Shrim Klim Namah Shivaya

Om and Salutations to Shiva and his—to the consciousness of the elements and the power that manifests this creation.

Goal Use this mantra to speed your attainment of the Siddha state. Adding the seed syllables *Shrim* and *Klim* to the great Siddha Mantra increases the access by our conscious mind to the primordial abundant creativity of *Shrim* and concentrates it through the syllable *Klim*.

Elements of the Mantra

Om The seed sound for the sixth (Ajna) chakra, from which the principle of mind directs all that follows.

Shrim The seed sound for abundance.

Klim The seed sound for attraction. It concentrates and attracts those things that surround it.

Namah Shivaya *Na Ma Shi Va Ya* are sounds that invoke conscious control over the elements which rule the chakras—namely earth, water, fire, air, and ether. Collectively, they are referred to as Shiva—the consciousness of all creation.

To the traditional Siddha Mantra, *Om Namah Shivaya,* some scriptures add certain seed sounds for accelerated progression toward the siddha state. This version is taught in conjunction with the *Shiva Kavacha,* or protective armor of Shiva.

The *Maha Lakshmi Astakam* affirms that Lakshmi is certainly the spouse of Vishnu, but it also proclaims that she is the shakti of Shiva himself. This means that Lakshmi takes the form of Parvati as Shiva's spouse in the myths pertaining to them. The basic Siddha Mantra is, therefore, augmented by the vibrations of manifestation and attraction. Spiritual freedom, or *Moksha,* is implied as a natural accompaniment to being a Siddha.

OTHER MANTRAS FOR MOKSHA

The Gayatri Mantra (page 57)

The Gayatri Mantra, previously discussed, is also a Moksha Mantra. It will bestow every attainment, including liberation, if practiced faithfully.

The Great Mani Mantra (page 59)

Practiced with dedication for release from spiritual bondage, the Mani Mantra will lead to the state of Moksha.

CHAPTER
TEN

A Feng Shui Mantra for Clearing Negative Energies

FENG SHUI is the study of the various types of energy and how they flow in one's living and working surroundings. As a student of Feng Shui, I have a working knowledge of the divisions within one's home or work space as taught by a master *Black Hat* (Tibetan) Feng Shui practitioner and teacher, Nathan Batoon. For his workshops, I have taught mantras that relate to space and the elements in nature that strongly influence events and situations in our life. The following Feng Shui mantra for clearing a space or environment of negative energies is particularly useful in creating a sacred space, such as the space where you intend to do your meditations.

MANTRA FOR CLEARING A SPACE OR ENVIRONMENT
Hung Vajra Pay
By the Power of Phat and Hum, let negativity leave this environment.

LISTEN TO TRACK 15
Hung Vajra Pay Mantra

Goal Use this mantra for clearing a space or environment of negative energies.

Elements of the Mantra

Hung The Tibetan pronunciation of the Sanskrit term, *Hum*, seed sound for the *Vishuddha* (throat) chakra. This seed sound is so powerful in repelling unwanted vibrations it is commonly called a "weapon mantra."

Vajra Thunderbolt, indicating the power of the mind to penetrate any environment—material, mental, or emotional.

Pay Tibetan pronunciation for the Sanskrit term *Phat*, another "weapon" seed sound that repels unwanted vibrations.

In 1982, I received the Vajrapani Empowerment from Sakya Jetsun Chiney Luding, commonly known as Jetsun Ma. Vajrapani is "He who protects followers of the dharma and is the Great Initiator." His simple mantra, *Hung Vajra Pay,* can bring a most powerful and beautiful light into any space.

I had practiced the mantra only intermittently for a couple of years. Then one day, as I was clearing debris and junk from the garage, I decided that it needed to be cleaned spiritually as well as physically. *The Hung Vajra Pay* mantra came to mind. As I cleaned the garage for the next three hours, I softly chanted the mantra. When I had finished, I went back into the house to do some work in the kitchen. After about ten minutes, I realized that I needed a tool from the garage. Opening the door from the kitchen, I entered and stopped dead in my tracks and listened. What I heard was the thick kind of silence.

I realized that there must have been years of background chatter or noise vibrations stored in the recesses of the walls. The chanting of mantra for three hours had reduced the background noise to zero. The effect of the chanting was particularly striking because it existed in the garage, but nowhere else, because my intention was solely directed toward the area of the garage. Even days later, whenever I entered the garage, a palpable quiet would greet me.

About three years later, I had an opportunity to test this mantra again. When Mr. Sharma (not his real name) called, he had to struggle to get his story out to me over the phone. After pooling their savings of many years, he and his wife were able to purchase a four-unit apartment complex in a pleasant neighborhood in Southern California. Soon after completing their purchase, they left the units in care of one of the residents, whom they had hired to act as a manager during a trip to India to deal with pressing family matters. Three months later, they returned to find that the manager had left, and the new manager was a drug dealer. All of the units were now occupied by drug users. After expensive legal battles, they had managed to dislodge the manager and the tenants, and the units now stood empty.

They soon realized that the units had not only a bad reputation, but a terrible psychic environment as well. They needed to have the place cleaned of all of the accumulated negative energies it had attracted, and called me, wondering if I could help.

I told them that I could do something, and that it would take a whole day, since I would need to chant in every room for a certain period of time, and scheduled a "cleaning session."

I chanted for about twenty minutes in each room of every unit, which took about six hours. I also circumambulated the entire property while chanting an ancient Vedic hymn, and shortly afterwards, the units rented quickly with normal, mainstream tenants, and the owners were extremely pleased.

CHAPTER
ELEVEN

Beginning Your First Mantra Practice

IN THIS PROGRAM, you have been introduced to fourteen mantras and how to use them. You probably already have some idea about which area you need to focus on. Begin by choosing one mantra and committing to a discipline. If you choose to use a mala, you can probably find one by doing a search on the Internet, or at a local store selling imports from India or Tibet. If you would like to create a special area of your house for your meditations, you can begin with the *Hung Vajra Pay* mantra on page 71 to cleanse the area for your spiritual practice. If you would like to create an altar, choose items that are meaningful to you. Be sure to sit in a posture in which you will remain comfortable for the length of time necessary to complete your practice. Listen to the CD at first to learn the correct pronunciation, and after that, you can continue to use the CD, or practice on your own. I usually recommend you start with one mantra for a forty-day discipline, but if you are eager to attain Mantra Siddhi, you can certainly do so. Using only one mantra for your first experiment will give you a clearer idea of how the mantra and the discipline works.

CHAPTER
TWELVE

Good Fortune to You

MAY YOU BE BLESSED with abundance that fills your cup until it is running over. In the process, it is my hope that you will be a shining example for your community, donating to worthy causes with your abundance and your time.

May your noble desires be fulfilled, bringing you joy and deep satisfaction. Being fulfilled yourself, may a path be shown to you for helping others also reach some kind of fulfillment.

May you support that personal swadharma that will lead to great reduction in your karmic obligations. At the same time, may your efforts work to restore dharma on the earth for all people.

May you achieve the jewel of Moksha, bringing with it the true spiritual freedom that your spirit has long sought. If it is consistent with your spirit and the blueprint of your soul, may you choose the path of Earth Service, helping guide humanity to its grand destiny and the Earth to reach the spiritual pinnacle of her own evolutionary path.

I intuitively know that as you engage with this program, you will be inspired to peruse several of the mantra meditation practices described. Some you will complete fairly soon, while others will be undertaken later. But you will experiment. You will help yourself, humanity, and the planet itself through your efforts. So I thank you and I salute you. May God attend your every need.

In Service,
Thomas Ashley-Farrand
(Namadeva)

BOOKS

Ashley-Farrand, Thomas. *Healing Mantras*. New York, NY: Ballantine Wellspring Books, 1999.

———. *Shakti Mantras*. New York, NY: Ballantine Books, 2003.

———. *True Stories of Spiritual Power*. Pasadena, CA: Saraswati Publications, LLC, 1995, 2001 (available at www.sanskritmantra.com).

———. *The Ancient Science of Sanskrit Mantra and Ceremony (Vols I-III)*. Pasadena, CA: Saraswati Publications, LLC, 1995, 2001 (available at www.sanskritmantra.com).

Blavatsky, H.P. *The Secret Doctrine, Vol I*. Pasadena, CA: Theosophical University Press, California, 1977.

Board of Scholars. *Mantramahoddadhi*. Delhi, India: Sri Satguru Publications, 1984.

Carter, Karen Rauch. *Move Your Stuff, Change Your Life*. New York, NY: Fireside Books, 2000.

Dowson, John. *A Classical Dctionary of Hindu Mythology and Religion, Geography, History and Literature*. New Delhi, India: D.K. Printworld, 1998, 2000.

Gupta, Sanjukta. *Laksmi Tantra*. Leiden, Netherlands: Brill, 1972.

Pargiter, F. Eden, B.A. *The Markandeya Purana*. Delhi, India: The Asiatic Society of Bengal, 1981.

Singh, Jaideva. *Shiva Sutras*. Delhi, India: Motilal Benarsidass, 1979, 1988.

Sivananda, Swami. *Sadhana*. U.P., Himalayas: Yoga Vedanta Forest Academy, The Divine Life Society, 1958.

Walker, Benjamin. *The Hindu World. (Vols. I and II)*. New York, NY: Frederick A. Praeger, 1968.

AUDIO PROGRAMS

Ashley-Farrand, Thomas. *Mantra: Sacred Words of Power*. Louisville, CO: Sounds True, 2000. Nine-hour class on audiocassette.

———. *Healing Mantras*. Louisville, CO: Sounds True, 2000. Compact disc.

———. *Mantra Meditation for Attracting Abundance*. Louisville, CO: Sounds True, 2003. Compact disc.

———. *Mantra Meditation for Attracting and Healing Relationships*. Louisville, CO: Sounds True, 2003. Compact disc.

———. *Mantra Meditation for Physical Health*. Louisville, CO: Sounds True, 2003. Compact disc.

———. *Mantra Therapy*. Pasadena, CA: Saraswati Publications, LLC, 2001. 2 Compact discs (available at www.sanskritmantra.com).

About the Author

THOMAS ASHLEY-FARRAND (Namadeva) has practiced mantra-based spiritual disciplines since 1973, and is an acknowledged expert in Sanskrit Mantra spiritual disciplines and ceremonies

He has received initiations and blessings from a number of prominent spiritual teachers, including Jagadguru Shankaracharya Jayendra Saraswati of Kanchi Math, the Madvacharya lineage Jagadguru of Pejowar Math, the Dalai Lama, the 16th Gyalwa Karmapa, Kalu Rimpoche, Sakya Jetsun Chiney Luding, and Christian mystic Dr. Leon Wright. His guru is Sadguru Sant Keshavadas (now deceased) from Bangalore, India. He follows Guru Mata, Sata Keshavadas' widow to whom he transferred spiritual authority on the banks of the Ganges before his passing.

Vedic Priest, author, and international lecturer and storyteller, Mr. Ashley-Farrand has given workshops and made presentations in the U.S. and Canada as well as India. He was a priest for the Temple of Cosmic Religion in Washington, DC, and has taught at George Washington University and Chaffee College.

He is president of Sanatana Dharma Satsang, a Kriya Yoga Initiate, and a member of Astara. Thomas currently lives in southern California with his wife Satyabhama, an attorney in private practice who often performs the ancient Vedic ceremonies with him.

SOUNDS TRUE was founded in 1985 by Tami Simon, with a clear vision: to disseminate spiritual wisdom. Located in Boulder, Colorado, Sounds True publishes teaching programs that are designed to educate, uplift, and inspire. With more than 600 titles available, we work with many of the leading spiritual teachers, thinkers, healers, and visionary artists of our time.

For a free catalog, or for more information on audio programs by Thomas Ashley-Farrand, please contact Sounds True via the World Wide Web at www.soundstrue.com, call us toll free at 800-333-9185, or write

The Sounds True Catalog
PO Box 8010
Boulder, CO 80306

CD SESSIONS

1. *The Esoteric Lakshmi Mantra* 5:00

2. *The Mantra of Kubera* 4:00

3. *A Shiva Mantra* 4:00

4. *A Ganesha/Ganapati Mantra* 6:00

5. *Aham Prema Mantra* 4:00

6. *The Dhanvantre Mantra* 6:00

7. *The Great Mantra of Chamundi* 4:00

8. *The Gayatri Mantra* 12:00

9. *The Great Mani Mantra* 4:00

10. *The Dattatreya Mantra* 5:00

11. *The Vasudeva Mantra* 8:00

12. *Taraka Rama Mantra* 3:00

13. *Parameshwari Mantra* 5:00

14. *The Enhanced Siddha Mantra* 4:00

15. *Hung Vajra Pay Mantra* 3:00